Table of Contents

As Easy as 1–2–3

① **Prepare** the assessment task activity.

② **Administer** the task and record the student's performance.

③ **Reteach** or provide additional practice using the reproducible activity sheet.

Everything You Need

Each assessment task includes:

- **Scripted instructions**
  for administering the assessment task

- **Full-color mats and cards**
  to engage the student in a specific task

- **Class checklist**
  to record each student's performance

- **Reproducible activity sheets**
  for additional skill practice

When to Conduct an Assessment

You may choose to use assessment tasks in any of the following ways:

- Assess students at the beginning of the school year to determine individual student skill levels.

- Administer an assessment after a specific skill has been taught to help confirm mastery or need for further instruction.

- Assess students throughout the year to monitor progress. Use the correlation chart on page 6 to correlate assessments with your lesson plans.

You may also wish to visit www.teaching-standards.com to view how the skills are correlated to your state's standards.

School Year _____	Correlation Chart		
Skill			
Concepts of Print/Print Awareness		**Week**	**Lesson**
Distinguishes Letters from Words			
Demonstrates Alphabet Recognition			
Identifies Front & Back Cover and Title Page			
Follows Words from Left to Right and Top to Bottom			
Understands That Printed Materials Provide Information			
Phonemic Awareness			
Identifies Beginning Sounds in an Alliterative Sentence			
Identifies and Produces Rhyming Words			
Identifies Beginning Consonant Sounds			
Identifies Medial Sounds			
Distinguishes Ending Consonant Sounds			
Blends Onsets and Rimes			
Segments Onsets and Rimes			
Oral Blending Phoneme by Phoneme			
Oral Segmentation Phoneme by Phoneme			
Counts Syllables in Words			
Phonics and Word Recognition			
Identifies Consonant Names and Sounds			
Matches Short Vowel Sound to the Letter			
Matches Beginning Sound to the Correct Letter			
Reads High-Frequency and CVC Words			
Vocabulary & Concept Development			
Understands Story Structure			
Sorts Items into Categories			

6

EMC 3337 • Reading Assessment Tasks • © Evan-Moor Corp.

Preparing an Assessment Task Activity

Assemble each assessment task activity and place it in an envelope. Store the envelopes in a file box or crate for easy access.

Materials:

- 9" x 12" (23 x 30.5 cm) large manila envelopes
- scissors
- clear tape
- scripted instructions, manipulatives, class checklist, and activity sheet for the specific assessment task

Steps to Follow:

1. Remove and laminate the *scripted instruction page*. Tape it to the front of the envelope.

2. Remove and laminate the *manipulatives* (sorting mats, task cards, etc.). Store cards in a smaller envelope or plastic bag.

3. Reproduce the *class checklist*. Tape it to the back of the envelope.

4. Make multiple copies of the *activity sheet* and store them in the envelope.

Make one copy of the *Individual Student Assessment Checklist* (page 5) for each student in your class. You may wish to keep these checklists in a separate binder so they are easily referenced.

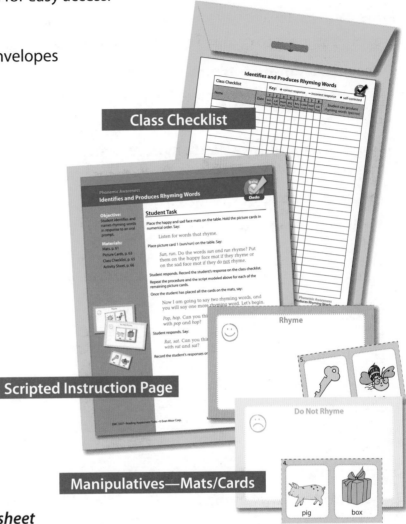

Class Checklist

Scripted Instruction Page

Manipulatives—Mats/Cards

Activity Sheet

How to Conduct an Assessment

- **Be prepared.**

  Preread the scripted instructions. Follow the directions at the top of the script for setting out the cards and mats. Have the class checklist at hand to record the student's responses. Do not ask the student to come to the table until all task materials are in place.

- **Provide a non-threatening atmosphere.**

  The student should complete the task at a quiet, isolated table. Refer to the activity as a "task" or "job," not as a "test."

- **Provide a non-distracting environment.**

  The student should be able to easily focus on the task. Sit next to the student. Communicate in a clear, concise way.

- **Be an unbiased assessor.**

  Do not encourage or discourage or approve or disapprove of the student's responses. Be careful not to use facial expressions that provide feedback.

- **Know when to stop the assessment.**

  Discontinue the assessment activity if it becomes obvious that the student cannot do the task.

- **Be discreet.**

  When recording the student's responses, keep the checklist close to you so it will not distract the student.

What does this mean?

/p/   When a letter is between / /, the letter sound, not the letter name, should be pronounced.

c•at   When a bullet appears within a word, emphasize each word part separately.

(◡)   is used to represent short vowel sounds: căt, gĕt, ĭt, hŏt, pŭp.

(—)   is used to represent long vowel sounds: cāke, mē, bīte, hōme, ūse.

 Some tasks are auditory only, and are indicated by this icon on the teacher script page. Auditory tasks do not contain mats or task cards.

Quick Checks

Unit 1
Concepts of Print/Print Awareness

Distinguishes Letters from Words

Objective:
Student discriminates between letters and words.

Materials:
Letter Mat, p. 11

Word Mat, p. 13

Letter and Word Cards, p. 15

Class Checklist, p. 17

Activity Sheet, p. 18

Model the Task

Spread the letter cards and the word cards faceup on the table. Place the letter mat and the word mat on the table. Say:

> Today we will decide if a card shows only a letter or a whole word.

Point to each mat as you say:

> Letter cards belong here and word cards belong here.

Choose a word card and place it on the word mat. Say:

> This card shows a word. So it belongs on the word mat.

Student Task

> Now you choose a card.

Student responds. Say:

> Does it show a letter or a word?

Student responds. Say:

> Place it on the correct mat.

Student responds. Say:

> Now look at the cards one at a time and place them on the letter mat or the word mat.

Student places all the cards on a mat. Once the student has placed all the cards, record the student's responses on the class checklist.

Letter Mat

Aa Bb Cc

Distinguishes Letters from Words

Concepts of Print/Print Awareness

EMC 3337 • © Evan-Moor Corp.

Word Mat

boy   cat   sun

Concepts of Print/Print Awareness
Distinguishes Letters from Words   **13**

Distinguishes Letters from Words

EMC 3337 • © Evan-Moor Corp.

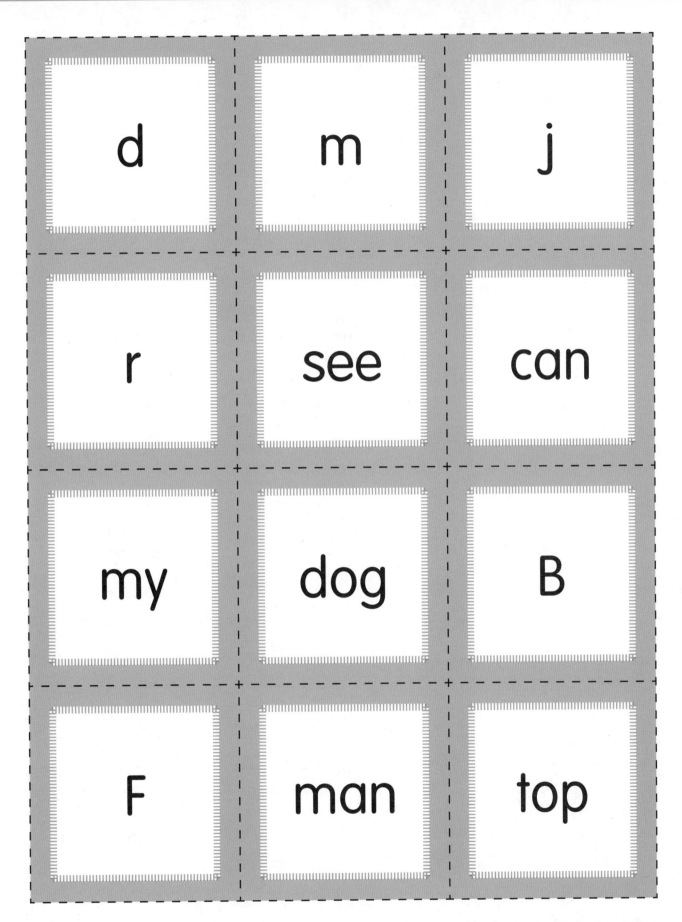

**Distinguishes
Letters from Words**

Concepts of Print/
Print Awareness

EMC 3337 • © Evan-Moor Corp.

**Distinguishes
Letters from Words**

Concepts of Print/
Print Awareness

EMC 3337 • © Evan-Moor Corp.

**Distinguishes
Letters from Words**

Concepts of Print/
Print Awareness

EMC 3337 • © Evan-Moor Corp.

**Distinguishes
Letters from Words**

Concepts of Print/
Print Awareness

EMC 3337 • © Evan-Moor Corp.

**Distinguishes
Letters from Words**

Concepts of Print/
Print Awareness

EMC 3337 • © Evan-Moor Corp.

**Distinguishes
Letters from Words**

Concepts of Print/
Print Awareness

EMC 3337 • © Evan-Moor Corp.

**Distinguishes
Letters from Words**

Concepts of Print/
Print Awareness

EMC 3337 • © Evan-Moor Corp.

**Distinguishes
Letters from Words**

Concepts of Print/
Print Awareness

EMC 3337 • © Evan-Moor Corp.

**Distinguishes
Letters from Words**

Concepts of Print/
Print Awareness

EMC 3337 • © Evan-Moor Corp.

**Distinguishes
Letters from Words**

Concepts of Print/
Print Awareness

EMC 3337 • © Evan-Moor Corp.

**Distinguishes
Letters from Words**

Concepts of Print/
Print Awareness

EMC 3337 • © Evan-Moor Corp.

**Distinguishes
Letters from Words**

Concepts of Print/
Print Awareness

EMC 3337 • © Evan-Moor Corp.

Distinguishes Letters from Words

Class Checklist		Key: + correct response − incorrect response ● self-corrected		
Name	Date	Distinguishes Letters	Distinguishes Words	Notes

Concepts of Print/Print Awareness

Name _____

Sort It

Cut. Match. Glue.

Aa Bb Cc	cat
glue	glue
glue	glue
glue	glue

man	R	k
bat	s	key

Demonstrates Alphabet Recognition

Objective:
Student names and matches capital and lowercase letters.

Materials:
Letter Cards, pp. 21–27

Class Checklist, p. 29

Activity Sheet, p. 30

Model the Task

Spread letter cards a–j faceup in random order on the table. Say:

> Look at the letter cards. There are uppercase letters and lowercase letters. I will match an uppercase letter to its lowercase letter.

Choose an uppercase letter and match it to its lowercase letter. Say the name of the letter aloud. Then as you fit them together, say:

> They fit together like a puzzle.

Student Task

> Now it's your turn. Put together an uppercase letter with its lowercase letter.

Student responds. Say:

> Which letters did you match?

Student responds. Say:

> Make another match. Tell me the name of the letter.

Student responds. Say:

> Match all of the uppercase and lowercase letter cards. Tell me each letter name as you match the cards.

Student names and matches all the cards at his or her own pace. Once the letter pairs are matched, place letter cards k–t on the table. The student will continue to match the letter pairs. Once he or she has matched all the letter cards, place letter cards u–z on the table. Record letters the student incorrectly names or matches on the class checklist.

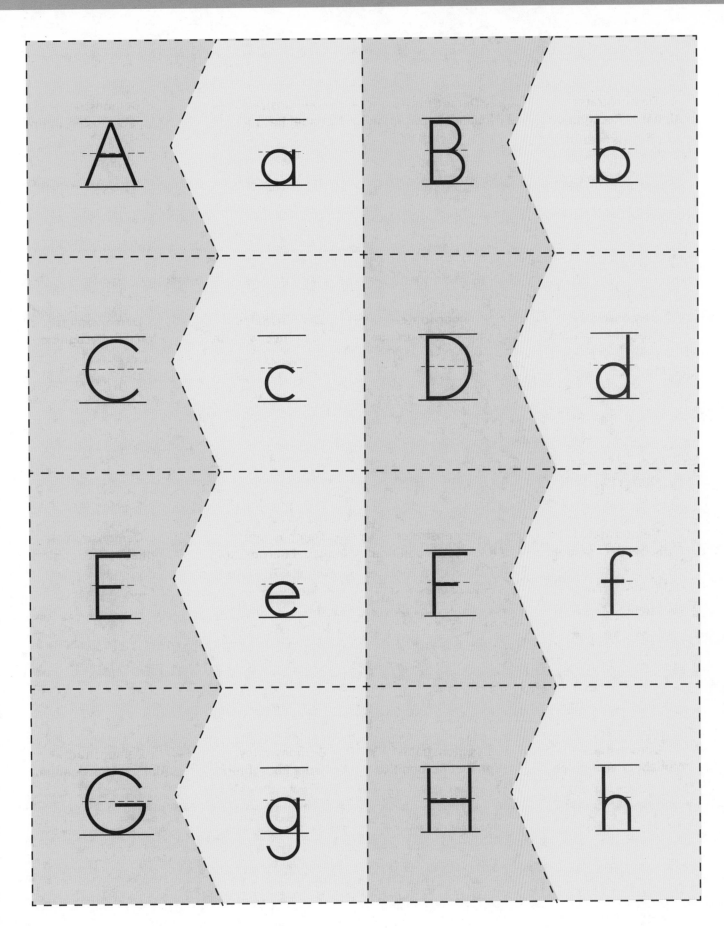

**Demonstrates
Alphabet Recognition**

Concepts of Print/
Print Awareness

EMC 3337 • © Evan-Moor Corp.

**Demonstrates
Alphabet Recognition**

Concepts of Print/
Print Awareness

EMC 3337 • © Evan-Moor Corp.

**Demonstrates
Alphabet Recognition**

Concepts of Print/
Print Awareness

EMC 3337 • © Evan-Moor Corp.

**Demonstrates
Alphabet Recognition**

Concepts of Print/
Print Awareness

EMC 3337 • © Evan-Moor Corp.

**Demonstrates
Alphabet Recognition**

Concepts of Print/
Print Awareness

EMC 3337 • © Evan-Moor Corp.

**Demonstrates
Alphabet Recognition**

Concepts of Print/
Print Awareness

EMC 3337 • © Evan-Moor Corp.

**Demonstrates
Alphabet Recognition**

Concepts of Print/
Print Awareness

EMC 3337 • © Evan-Moor Corp.

**Demonstrates
Alphabet Recognition**

Concepts of Print/
Print Awareness

EMC 3337 • © Evan-Moor Corp.

**Demonstrates
Alphabet Recognition**

Concepts of Print/
Print Awareness

EMC 3337 • © Evan-Moor Corp.

**Demonstrates
Alphabet Recognition**

Concepts of Print/
Print Awareness

EMC 3337 • © Evan-Moor Corp..

**Demonstrates
Alphabet Recognition**

Concepts of Print/
Print Awareness

EMC 3337 • © Evan-Moor Corp.

**Demonstrates
Alphabet Recognition**

Concepts of Print/
Print Awareness

EMC 3337 • © Evan-Moor Corp.

**Demonstrates
Alphabet Recognition**

Concepts of Print/
Print Awareness

EMC 3337 • © Evan-Moor Corp.

**Demonstrates
Alphabet Recognition**

Concepts of Print/
Print Awareness

EMC 3337 • © Evan-Moor Corp.

**Demonstrates
Alphabet Recognition**

Concepts of Print/
Print Awareness

EMC 3337 • © Evan-Moor Corp.

**Demonstrates
Alphabet Recognition**

Concepts of Print/
Print Awareness

EMC 3337 • © Evan-Moor Corp.

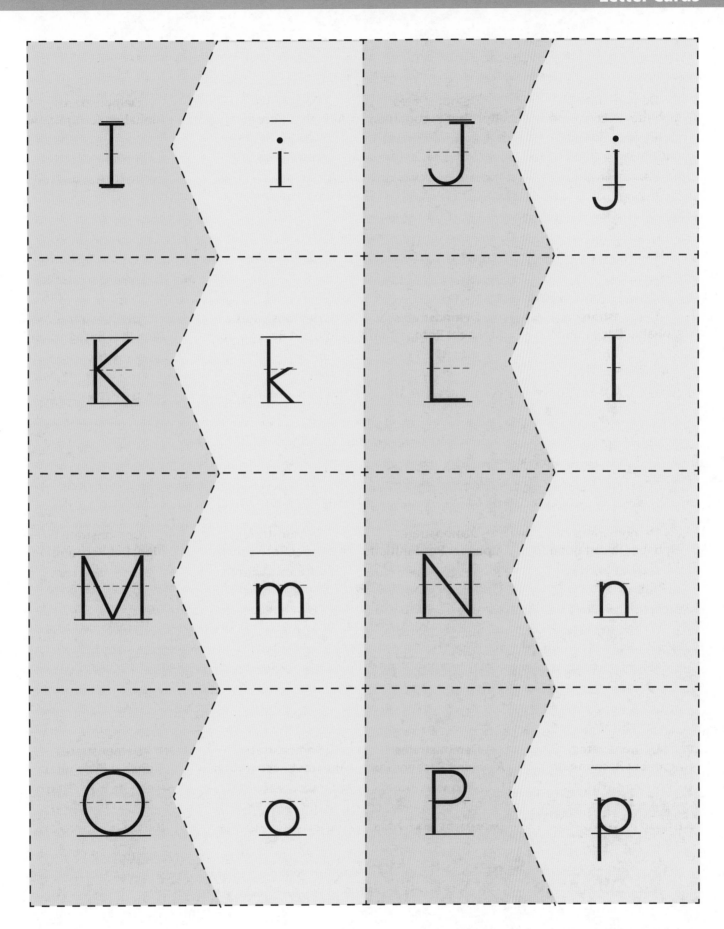

Demonstrates
Alphabet Recognition
Concepts of Print/
Print Awareness

EMC 3337 • © Evan-Moor Corp.

Demonstrates
Alphabet Recognition
Concepts of Print/
Print Awareness

EMC 3337 • © Evan-Moor Corp.

Demonstrates
Alphabet Recognition
Concepts of Print/
Print Awareness

EMC 3337 • © Evan-Moor Corp.

Demonstrates
Alphabet Recognition
Concepts of Print/
Print Awareness

EMC 3337 • © Evan-Moor Corp.

Demonstrates
Alphabet Recognition
Concepts of Print/
Print Awareness

EMC 3337 • © Evan-Moor Corp.

Demonstrates
Alphabet Recognition
Concepts of Print/
Print Awareness

EMC 3337 • © Evan-Moor Corp.

Demonstrates
Alphabet Recognition
Concepts of Print/
Print Awareness

EMC 3337 • © Evan-Moor Corp.

Demonstrates
Alphabet Recognition
Concepts of Print/
Print Awareness

EMC 3337 • © Evan-Moor Corp.

Demonstrates
Alphabet Recognition
Concepts of Print/
Print Awareness

EMC 3337 • © Evan-Moor Corp.

Demonstrates
Alphabet Recognition
Concepts of Print/
Print Awareness

EMC 3337 • © Evan-Moor Corp..

Demonstrates
Alphabet Recognition
Concepts of Print/
Print Awareness

EMC 3337 • © Evan-Moor Corp.

Demonstrates
Alphabet Recognition
Concepts of Print/
Print Awareness

EMC 3337 • © Evan-Moor Corp.

Demonstrates
Alphabet Recognition
Concepts of Print/
Print Awareness

EMC 3337 • © Evan-Moor Corp.

Demonstrates
Alphabet Recognition
Concepts of Print/
Print Awareness

EMC 3337 • © Evan-Moor Corp.

Demonstrates
Alphabet Recognition
Concepts of Print/
Print Awareness

EMC 3337 • © Evan-Moor Corp.

Demonstrates
Alphabet Recognition
Concepts of Print/
Print Awareness

EMC 3337 • © Evan-Moor Corp.

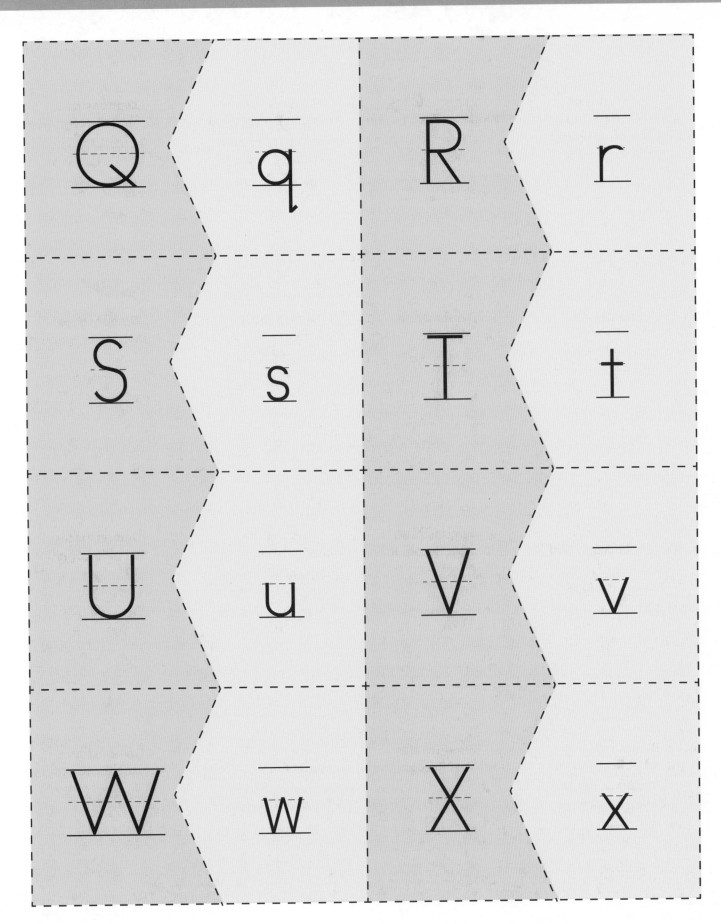

Concepts of Print/Print Awareness
Demonstrates Alphabet Recognition   **25**

**Demonstrates
Alphabet Recognition**

Concepts of Print/
Print Awareness

EMC 3337 • © Evan-Moor Corp.

**Demonstrates
Alphabet Recognition**

Concepts of Print/
Print Awareness

EMC 3337 • © Evan-Moor Corp.

**Demonstrates
Alphabet Recognition**

Concepts of Print/
Print Awareness

EMC 3337 • © Evan-Moor Corp.

**Demonstrates
Alphabet Recognition**

Concepts of Print/
Print Awareness

EMC 3337 • © Evan-Moor Corp.

**Demonstrates
Alphabet Recognition**

Concepts of Print/
Print Awareness

EMC 3337 • © Evan-Moor Corp.

**Demonstrates
Alphabet Recognition**

Concepts of Print/
Print Awareness

EMC 3337 • © Evan-Moor Corp.

**Demonstrates
Alphabet Recognition**

Concepts of Print/
Print Awareness

EMC 3337 • © Evan-Moor Corp.

**Demonstrates
Alphabet Recognition**

Concepts of Print/
Print Awareness

EMC 3337 • © Evan-Moor Corp.

**Demonstrates
Alphabet Recognition**

Concepts of Print/
Print Awareness

EMC 3337 • © Evan-Moor Corp.

**Demonstrates
Alphabet Recognition**

Concepts of Print/
Print Awareness

EMC 3337 • © Evan-Moor Corp..

**Demonstrates
Alphabet Recognition**

Concepts of Print/
Print Awareness

EMC 3337 • © Evan-Moor Corp.

**Demonstrates
Alphabet Recognition**

Concepts of Print/
Print Awareness

EMC 3337 • © Evan-Moor Corp.

**Demonstrates
Alphabet Recognition**

Concepts of Print/
Print Awareness

EMC 3337 • © Evan-Moor Corp.

**Demonstrates
Alphabet Recognition**

Concepts of Print/
Print Awareness

EMC 3337 • © Evan-Moor Corp.

**Demonstrates
Alphabet Recognition**

Concepts of Print/
Print Awareness

EMC 3337 • © Evan-Moor Corp.

**Demonstrates
Alphabet Recognition**

Concepts of Print/
Print Awareness

EMC 3337 • © Evan-Moor Corp.

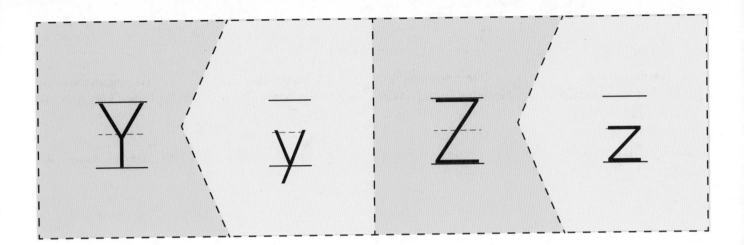

**Demonstrates
Alphabet Recognition**

Concepts of Print/
Print Awareness

EMC 3337 • © Evan-Moor Corp.

**Demonstrates
Alphabet Recognition**

Concepts of Print/
Print Awareness

EMC 3337 • © Evan-Moor Corp.

**Demonstrates
Alphabet Recognition**

Concepts of Print/
Print Awareness

EMC 3337 • © Evan-Moor Corp.

**Demonstrates
Alphabet Recognition**

Concepts of Print/
Print Awareness

EMC 3337 • © Evan-Moor Corp.

Demonstrates Alphabet Recognition

Class Checklist		Write all letters the student incorrectly named or matched.		
Name	Date	Incorrectly Named Letters	Incorrectly Matched Letters	Notes

Note: Student traces each letter.

Name _____

My Alphabet

Trace each letter.

Aa   Bb   Cc   Dd

Ee   Ff   Gg   Hh

Ii   Jj   Kk   Ll

Mm   Nn   Oo   Pp

Qq   Rr   Ss   Tt

Uu   Vv   Ww   Xx

Yy   Zz

Identifies Front & Back Cover and Title Page

Objective:
Student identifies the front cover, back cover, and title page of a book.

Materials:
Student Book: *Welcome to the Farm*, pp. 33–36

Class Checklist, p. 37

Activity Sheet, p. 38

Student Task

Place the book on the table. Point to the book. Say:

> Show me the front cover of the book.

Student responds by pointing to the front cover of the book. Say:

> Show me the back cover of the book.

Student responds by pointing to the back cover of the book. Say:

> Can you find the title page of the book?

Student responds by opening the book and pointing to the title page. Record the student's responses on the class checklist.

EMC 3337 • Reading Assessment Tasks • © Evan-Moor Corp.

Note: Laminate pages 33 and 35. Cut them out and fold. Place page 35 inside the folded page 33.

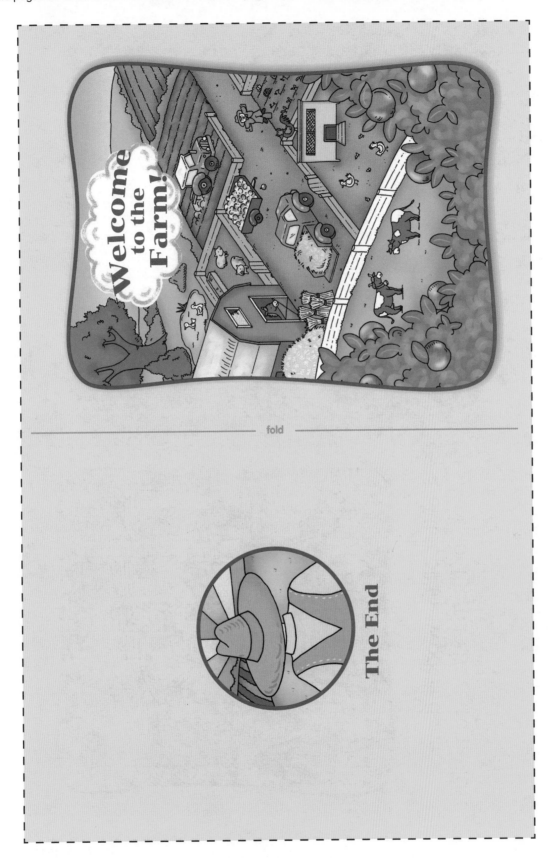

fold

Concepts of Print/Print Awareness
Identifies Front & Back Cover and Title Page **33**

fold

After all the work is done,
it's time for them to have some fun!

3

Welcome
to the
Farm!

by
Jo Ellen Moore

Illustrated by
Mary Rojas

fold

People live and work on a farm.

2

Concepts of Print/Print Awareness
Identifies Front & Back Cover and Title Page   **35**

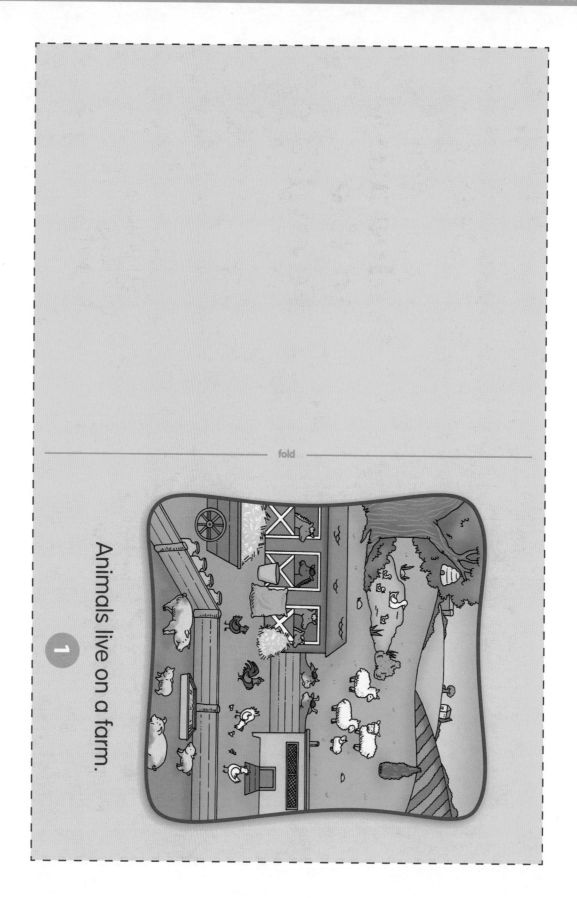

1

Animals live on a farm.

Identifies Front & Back Cover and Title Page

Class Checklist		Key:	**+** correct response	**−** incorrect response	**●** self-corrected

Name	Date	Identifies Front Cover	Identifies Back Cover	Identifies Title Page	Notes

Note: An adult makes the book by cutting and folding the paper on the lines indicated.

Name _____

My Own Little Book

2

I see a pig.

fold 1

I see a cow.

1

fold 2

I
Can
See

3

I see a hen.

fold 1

The
End

fold 2

I
Can
See

by
Farmer Joe

I
Can
See

Follows Words from Left to Right and Top to Bottom

Objective:

Student tracks words from left to right and top to bottom.

Materials:

Mat, p. 41

Class Checklist, p. 43

Activity Sheet, p. 44

Student Task

Place the mat on the table. Say:

> Look at the story. Point to where I begin reading.

Student responds. Say:

> Run your finger over the words as I read.

Read the first sentence to the student. Student responds. (You are looking for the student to demonstrate left-to-right tracking.) Say:

> Now point to where I read next.

Read the second sentence to the student. Student responds. (You are looking for the student to demonstrate top-to-bottom directionality.)

Finish reading the story to the student.

Record the student's responses on the class checklist.

40 **Follows Words from Left to Right and Top to Bottom**

Oink! Oink!

Oink! Oink! Oink!

I see three pigs.

Oink! Oink! Oink!

Pigs like mud.

**Follows Words from Left to Right
and Top to Bottom**
Concepts of Print/Print Awareness

EMC 3337 • © Evan-Moor Corp.

Follows Words from Left to Right and Top to Bottom

Class Checklist		Key: + correct response − incorrect response ● self-corrected		
Name	Date	Follows Words Left to Right	Follows Words Top to Bottom	Notes

Concepts of Print/Print Awareness

Name _____

Oink! Oink!

Color the picture.

Oink! Oink! Oink!

I see three pigs.

Oink! Oink! Oink!

Pigs like mud.

Understands That Printed Materials Provide Information

Quick
Checks

Objective:

Student demonstrates an understanding that printed materials provide information.

Materials:

Mat 1, p. 47

Mat 2, p. 49

Class Checklist, p. 51

Activity Sheet, p. 52

Student Task

Place mat 1 or mat 2 on the table. Say:

> Look at the picture. Tell me what you think the words tell us about the picture.

Student responds. Record the student's response on the class checklist. An answer that draws clues from the picture is recorded as a correct response.

Say:

> Now listen as I read the words.

Read the story to the student. Then say:

Mat 1:

> What did you learn about elephants?

Mat 2:

> What did you learn about frogs?

Elephants Like Water

I see a big elephant.

I see a little elephant.

I see two elephants in the water.

Elephants like water.

Understands That Printed Materials Provide Information

Concepts of Print/Print Awareness

EMC 3337 • © Evan-Moor Corp.

Frogs Like Water

It is raining.

The rain makes puddles.

I see a frog in a puddle.

I am in a puddle, too!

Frogs like water.

Understands That Printed Materials Provide Information

Concepts of Print/Print Awareness

EMC 3337 • © Evan-Moor Corp.

Understands That Printed Materials Provide Information

Class Checklist				Key: + correct response – incorrect response ● self-corrected

Name	Date	Mat 1 Student's Response	Mat 2 Student's Response	Notes

Concepts of Print/Print Awareness

Name _____

Activity Sheet

A Pet

I have a pet.

Its name is Sam.

It is long.

It has black and yellow stripes.

Draw a picture of Sam. Color it.

Quick

Checks

Unit 2
Phonemic Awareness

Identifies Beginning Sounds in an Alliterative Sentence

Objective:
Student identifies the common beginning sounds of words in an alliterative sentence.

Materials:
Class Checklist, p. 57

Activity Sheet, p. 58

Auditory Only

Model the Task

Say:

> I am going to read a sentence. Listen carefully for the beginning sound in each word.

Emphasize the /s/ sound when reading the sentence. Say:

> *Silly Sally saw a snake.*

Say:

> I hear /s/ at the beginning of the words. Listen again. *Silly Sally saw a snake.*

Student Task

> Now I am going to read another sentence. Listen carefully for the beginning sound in each word.

> *Peter polishes pots and pans.* What sound did you hear at the beginning of each word?

Student responds. Record the student's response on the class checklist. Say:

> Listen carefully to this sentence: *Lisa likes licking little lollipops.* What sound did you hear at the beginning of each word?

Student responds. Record the student's response on the class checklist. Say:

> Listen carefully to this sentence: *Mary Maid makes many mistakes.* What sound did you hear at the beginning of each word?

Student responds. Record the student's response on the class checklist.

Identifies Beginning Sounds in an Alliterative Sentence

Class Checklist		Key:	+ correct response	− incorrect response	● self-corrected		
Name	Date	/p/	/l/	/m/	Notes		

Note: Read the sentence to the student. Student counts how many times he or she heard the sound of *s*.

Activity Sheet

Name _____

Listen for the Sound

Listen to the sentence.
Color the picture.

Silly Sally saw a snake.

How many times did you hear the sound of **s**? ☐

Phonemic Awareness

58 Identifies Beginning Sounds in an Alliterative Sentence   EMC 3337 • Reading Assessment Tasks • © Evan-Moor Corp.

Objective:

Student identifies and names rhyming words in response to an oral prompt.

Materials:

Mats, p. 61

Picture Cards, p. 63

Class Checklist, p. 65

Activity Sheet, p. 66

Student Task

Place the happy and sad face mats on the table. Hold the picture cards in numerical order. Say:

> Listen for words that rhyme.

Place picture card 1 (sun/run) on the table. Say:

> *Sun, run.* Do the words *sun* and *run* rhyme? Put them on the happy face mat if they rhyme or on the sad face mat if they do <u>not</u> rhyme.

Student responds. Record the student's response on the class checklist.

Repeat the procedure and the script modeled above for each of the remaining picture cards.

Once the student has placed all the cards on the mats, say:

> Now I am going to say two rhyming words, and you will say one more rhyming word. Let's begin.
>
> *Pop, hop.* Can you think of a word that rhymes with *pop* and *hop*?

Student responds. Say:

> *Rat, sat.* Can you think of a word that rhymes with *rat* and *sat*?

Record the student's responses on the class checklist.

Rhyming Words

Rhyme

Do Not Rhyme

Phonemic Awareness
Identifies and Produces Rhyming Words **61**

Identifies and Produces Rhyming Words

Phonemic Awareness

EMC 3337 • © Evan-Moor Corp.

Identifies and Produces Rhyming Words

Phonemic Awareness

EMC 3337 • © Evan-Moor Corp.

Rhyming Words

1. sun   run
2. cat   hat
3. man   can
4. pig   box
5. key   bee
6. cow   cup
7. tree   rug
8. car   bus

Identifies and Produces Rhyming Words

Phonemic Awareness

EMC 3337 • © Evan-Moor Corp.

Identifies and Produces Rhyming Words

Phonemic Awareness

EMC 3337 • © Evan-Moor Corp.

Identifies and Produces Rhyming Words

Phonemic Awareness

EMC 3337 • © Evan-Moor Corp.

Identifies and Produces Rhyming Words

Phonemic Awareness

EMC 3337 • © Evan-Moor Corp.

Identifies and Produces Rhyming Words

Phonemic Awareness

EMC 3337 • © Evan-Moor Corp.

Identifies and Produces Rhyming Words

Phonemic Awareness

EMC 3337 • © Evan-Moor Corp.

Identifies and Produces Rhyming Words

Phonemic Awareness

EMC 3337 • © Evan-Moor Corp.

Identifies and Produces Rhyming Words

Phonemic Awareness

EMC 3337 • © Evan-Moor Corp.

Identifies and Produces Rhyming Words

Class Checklist		Key: + correct response − incorrect response ● self-corrected									
Name	**Date**	**1** sun run	**2** cat hat	**3** man can	**4** pig box	**5** key bee	**6** cow cup	**7** tree rug	**8** car bus	**Student can produce rhyming words. (yes/no)**

Phonemic Awareness

Quick
Checks ✓

Activity Sheet

Name _____

Do I Rhyme?

Listen. Circle the two pictures in each row that rhyme.

1.

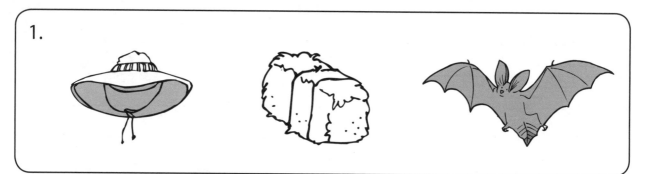

2.

3.

4.

Identifies Beginning Consonant Sounds

Objective:
Student listens to an oral prompt to identify beginning consonant sounds.

Materials:
Mat, p. 69
Class Checklist, p. 71
Activity Sheet, p. 72

Student Task

Place the mat on the table. Point to each picture as you say its name aloud. Say:

> Look at row 1. Listen for the two words that begin with the same sound.
>
> *Moon, mouse, sock.*
>
> Which two words begin with the same sound?

Student responds. Record the student's response on the class checklist. Point to row 2. Say:

> Look at row 2. Listen for the two words that begin with the same sound.
>
> *Lock, six, sun.*
>
> Which two words begin with the same sound?

Student responds. Record the student's response on the class checklist. Point to row 3. Say:

> Look at row 3. Listen for the two words that begin with the same sound.
>
> *Fox, fish, bike.*
>
> Which two words begin with the same sound?

Student responds. Record the student's response on the class checklist.

Repeat the procedure and the script modeled above for each of the remaining rows (ball, tiger, bus; turtle, tie, monkey).

Beginning Sounds

Identifies Beginning Consonant Sounds
Phonemic Awareness
EMC 3337 • © Evan-Moor Corp.

Identifies Beginning Consonant Sounds

Class Checklist							
Key: + correct response − incorrect response ● self-corrected							

Name	Date	Row 1 moon, mouse	Row 2 six, sun	Row 3 fox, fish	Row 4 ball, bus	Row 5 turtle, tie	Notes

Phonemic Awareness
Identifies Beginning Consonant Sounds

Activity Sheet

Name _____

Same Sound

Name each picture.
Circle the pictures in each row that begin with the same sound as the first one.

Identifies Medial Sounds

Objective:
Student listens to an oral prompt to identify medial sounds.

Materials:
Picture Cards, p. 75
Class Checklist, p. 77
Activity Sheet, p. 78

Model the Task

Place the picture cards in a pile on the table. Say:

> I will say a word. Listen for the middle sound.

Place the picture of the cat on the table. Say:

> Cat.

> I hear the /a/ sound in the middle of *cat*.

Student Task

Remove the cat picture card and place the cup picture card on the table. Say:

> Now I will say another word. Listen for the middle sound.

> Cup.

> Tell me the sound you hear in the middle.

Student responds. Record the student's response on the class checklist. Remove the cup picture card and place the pig picture card on the table. Say:

> Pig.

> Tell me the sound you hear in the middle.

Student responds. Record the student's response on the class checklist. Remove the pig picture card and place the bed picture card on the table.

Repeat the procedure and the script modeled above for each of the remaining picture cards (bed, fox, bag).

Phonemic Awareness
Identifies Medial Sounds

Medial Sounds

1.
2.
3.
4.
5.
6.

Phonemic Awareness
Identifies Medial Sounds

Identifies Medial Sounds

Phonemic Awareness

EMC 3337 • © Evan-Moor Corp.

Identifies Medial Sounds

Phonemic Awareness

EMC 3337 • © Evan-Moor Corp.

Identifies Medial Sounds

Phonemic Awareness

EMC 3337 • © Evan-Moor Corp.

Identifies Medial Sounds

Phonemic Awareness

EMC 3337 • © Evan-Moor Corp.

Identifies Medial Sounds

Phonemic Awareness

EMC 3337 • © Evan-Moor Corp.

Identifies Medial Sounds

Phonemic Awareness

EMC 3337 • © Evan-Moor Corp.

Identifies Medial Sounds

Class Checklist		Key: + correct response − incorrect response ● self-corrected						
Name	Date	/u/	/i/	/e/	/o/	/a/	Notes	

Activity Sheet

Name _____

Same Sound

Listen. Circle the picture in each row that has the same middle sound as the first one.

Phonemic Awareness
78 Identifies Medial Sounds

Distinguishes Ending Consonant Sounds

Objective:
Student listens to an oral prompt to distinguish ending sounds.

Materials:
Mat, p. 81

Class Checklist, p. 83

Activity Sheet, p. 84

Student Task

Place the mat on the table. Point to each picture as you say its name aloud. Say:

> Look at row 1. Listen for the two words that end with the same sound.
>
> *Cup, foot, boat.*
>
> Which two words end with the same sound?

Student responds. Record the student's response on the class checklist. Point to row 2 on the mat. Say:

> Look at row 2. Listen for the two words that end with the same sound.
>
> *Drum, pot, gum.*
>
> Which two words end with the same sound?

Student responds. Record the student's response on the class checklist. Point to row 3 on the mat. Say:

> Look at row 3. Listen for the two words that end with the same sound.
>
> *Sock, dog, lock.*
>
> Which two words end with the same sound?

Student responds. Record the student's response on the class checklist.

Repeat the procedure and the script modeled above for each of the remaining rows (bug, rug, pen; pig, star, four).

Ending Sounds

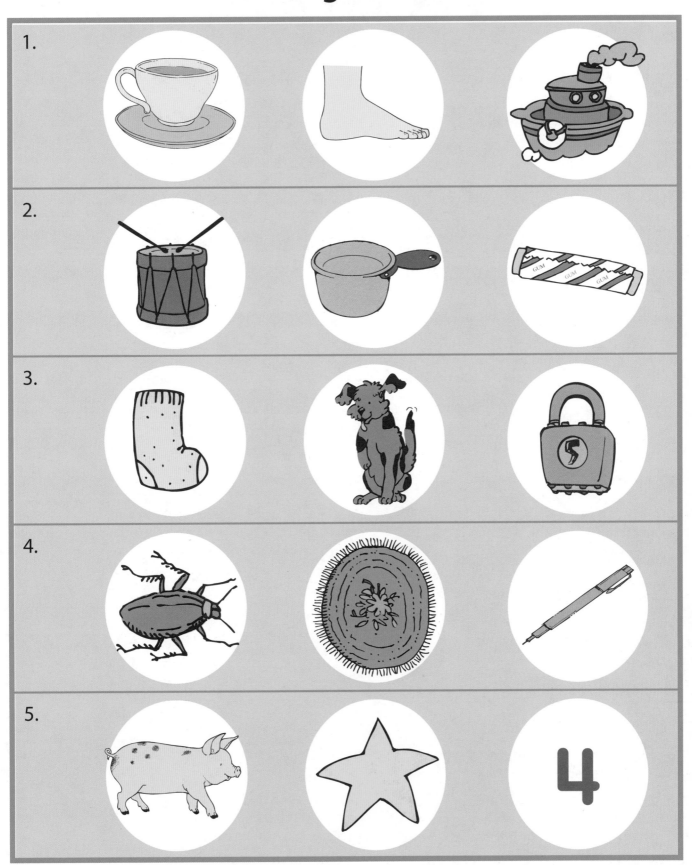

1.

2.

3.

4.

5.

Phonemic Awareness
Distinguishes Ending Consonant Sounds **81**

Distinguishes Ending Consonant Sounds

Phonemic Awareness

EMC 3337 • © Evan-Moor Corp.

Distinguishes Ending Consonant Sounds

Class Checklist		Key: + correct response − incorrect response ● self-corrected					

Name	Date	Row 1 foot, boat	Row 2 drum, gum	Row 3 sock, lock	Row 4 bug, rug	Row 5 star, four	Notes

Note: Student discriminates the ending sound in each word.
1. lip, pig. 2. star, four. 3. top, cup. 4. sock, lock. 5. coat, hat. 6. hive, ball.

Name _____

What Comes at the End?

Color 😊 if the pictures end with the same sound.

Color ☹ if the pictures do not end with the same sound.

1.

😊   ☹

2.

😊   ☹

3.

😊   ☹

4.

😊   ☹

5.

😊   ☹

6.

😊   ☹

Blends Onsets and Rimes

Objective:
Student listens to an onset and a rime and blends them into a whole word.

Onset: the consonants preceding the vowel of a syllable

Rime: the vowel of a syllable and any consonants that follow it

Materials:
Class Checklist, p. 87
Activity Sheet, p. 88

Auditory Only

Model the Task

Say:

> I will say two word parts and then say the word as a whole.
>
> /p/...an   The word is *pan*.

Student Task

> Now it's your turn.
> /s/...at   What is the word?

Student responds. Record the student's response on the class checklist. Say:

> /p/...en   What is the word?

Student responds. Record the student's response on the class checklist. Say:

> /h/...ug   What is the word?

Student responds. Record the student's response on the class checklist. Say:

> /t/...op   What is the word?

Student responds. Record the student's response on the class checklist. Say:

> /f/...in   What is the word?

Student responds. Record the student's response on the class checklist. Say:

> /j/...am   What is the word?

Student responds. Record the student's response on the class checklist.

Blends Onsets and Rimes

Class Checklist		Key:	+ correct response	− incorrect response	● self-corrected			
Name	Date	sat	pen	hug	top	fin	jam	Notes

Phonemic Awareness
Blends Onsets and Rimes **87**

Name _____

Follow Directions

Circle the picture that shows a /c/...at.
Underline the picture that shows a /d/...og.
Listen as I read the story.

The cat sees the dog.
The dog does <u>not</u> see the cat!

Segments Onsets and Rimes

Objective:

Student segments the onset and the rime of a given word.

Onset: the consonants preceding the vowel of a syllable

Rime: the vowel of a syllable and any consonants that follow it

Materials:

Picture Cards, p. 91

Class Checklist, p. 93

Activity Sheet, p. 94

Model the Task

Place the hat picture card on the table. Say:

> Today we will say the first sound in a word and then say the rest of the word. Listen closely.

hat /h•at/

Student Task

> Now you say the first sound in the word and then the rest of the word. Let's begin.

Place the van picture card on the table in front of the student. Say:

> *van*

Student responds. Record the student's response on the class checklist. Place the pin picture card on the table. Say:

> *pin*

Student responds. Record the student's response on the class checklist. Place the dog picture card on the table. Say:

> *dog*

Student responds. Record the student's response on the class checklist. Place the sun picture card on the table. Say:

> *sun*

Student responds. Record the student's response on the class checklist. Place the cat picture card on the table. Say:

> *cat*

Student responds. Record the student's response on the class checklist.

1.

2.

3.

4.

5.

6.

Segments Onsets and Rimes
Phonemic Awareness
EMC 3337 • © Evan-Moor Corp.

Segments Onsets and Rimes
Phonemic Awareness
EMC 3337 • © Evan-Moor Corp.

Segments Onsets and Rimes
Phonemic Awareness
EMC 3337 • © Evan-Moor Corp.

Segments Onsets and Rimes
Phonemic Awareness
EMC 3337 • © Evan-Moor Corp.

Segments Onsets and Rimes
Phonemic Awareness
EMC 3337 • © Evan-Moor Corp.

Segments Onsets and Rimes
Phonemic Awareness
EMC 3337 • © Evan-Moor Corp.

Segments Onsets and Rimes

Class Checklist							
Key: + correct response − incorrect response • self-corrected							

Name	Date	van: /v•an/	pin: /p•in/	dog: /d•og/	sun: /s•un/	cat: /c•at/	Notes

Phonemic Awareness

Name _____

Which Word?

I will say a word.
You say the first sound and then the rest of the word.

1. **hat**	2. **cup**
3. **pin**	4. **dog**
5. **cow**	6. **car**

Oral Blending Phoneme by Phoneme

Quick
Checks

Objective:
Student blends phonemes to make words.

Materials:
Class Checklist, p. 97

Activity Sheet, p. 98

**Auditory
Only**

Model the Task

Say:

> I am going to say three word parts. Then I will say the word as a whole. Listen.

> /c/ /u/ /t/   The word is *cut*.

Student Task

> Now it's your turn. Listen to the word parts and say the word as a whole. Let's begin.

> /b/ /e/ /d/   What is the word?

Student responds. Record the student's response on the class checklist. Say:

> /h/ /a/ /t/   What is the word?

Student responds. Record the student's response on the class checklist. Say:

> /m/ /a/ /p/   What is the word?

Student responds. Record the student's response on the class checklist. Say:

> /w/ /i/ /g/   What is the word?

Student responds. Record the student's response on the class checklist. Say:

> /p/ /o/ /t/   What is the word?

Student responds. Record the student's response on the class checklist. Say:

> /s/ /u/ /n/   What is the word?

Student responds. Record the student's response on the class checklist. Say:

> /p/ /o/ /p/   What is the word?

Student responds. Record the student's response on the class checklist.

Oral Blending Phoneme by Phoneme

Class Checklist		Key: **+** correct response **−** incorrect response **●** self-corrected							
Name	Date	bed	hat	map	wig	pot	sun	pop	Notes

Name _____

How Many Sounds?

Name each picture. Count the sounds in each word.
Fill in the circles to show how many you hear.

1. pie ○ ○ ○	2. pin ○ ○ ○
3. cat ○ ○ ○	4. bee ○ ○ ○
5. sun ○ ○ ○	6. duck ○ ○ ○
7. bat ○ ○ ○	8. car ○ ○ ○

Objective:
Student listens to a word and identifies which sounds make up the word.

Materials:
Mat, p. 101

Class Checklist, p. 103

Activity Sheet, p. 104

Model the Task

Place the mat on the table. Say:

> I will say a word. Then I will say it sound by sound. I will tell you how many sounds I hear.

Point to picture 1 (mad). Say:

> *Mad. /m/ /a/ /d/*
> I hear three sounds in the word *mad*.

Student Task

> Now it's your turn.

Point to picture 2 (net). Say:

> *Net.* Say *net* sound by sound.

Student responds. Say:

> How many sounds do you hear?

Student responds. Record the student's response on the class checklist.

Point to picture 3 (rocks). Say:

> *Rocks.* Say *rocks* sound by sound.

Student responds. Say:

> How many sounds do you hear?

Student responds. Record the student's response on the class checklist.

Repeat the procedure and the script modeled above for each of the remaining picture cards.

EMC 3337 • Reading Assessment Tasks • © Evan-Moor Corp.

Oral Segmentation Phoneme by Phoneme

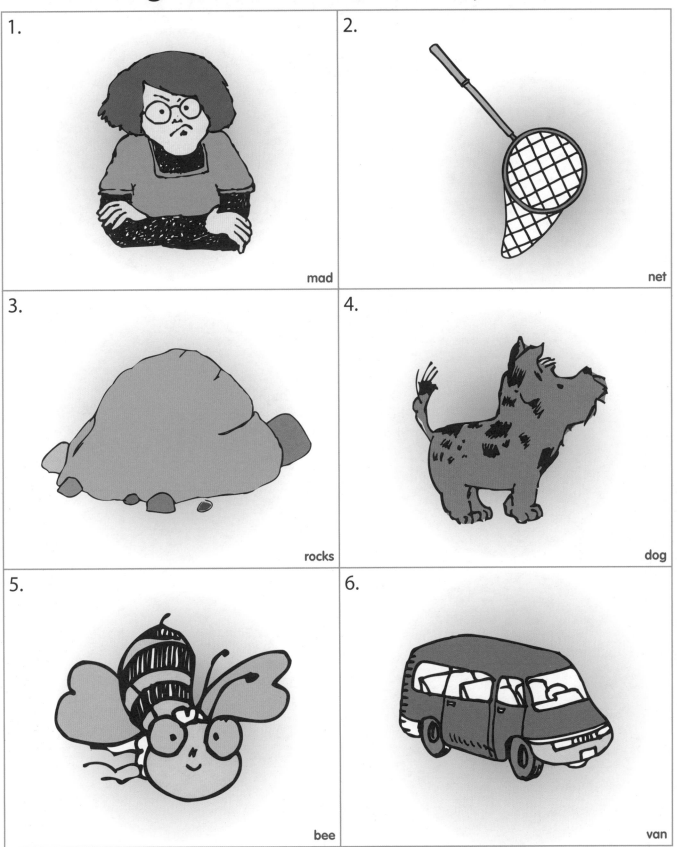

1.

mad

2.

net

3.

rocks

4.

dog

5.

bee

6.

van

**Oral Segmentation
Phoneme by Phoneme**
Phonemic Awareness

EMC 3337 • © Evan-Moor Corp.

Oral Segmentation Phoneme by Phoneme

Class Checklist		Key: + correct response − incorrect response ● self-corrected					
Name	Date	net (3)	rocks (4)	dog (3)	bee (2)	van (3)	Notes

Name _____

Listen and Count

Name each picture. Count the sounds you hear in each word.
Fill in the circles to show how many you hear.

1.	boat

◯ ◯ ◯ ◯

2.	bow

◯ ◯ ◯ ◯

3.	bus

◯ ◯ ◯ ◯

4.	book

MY BOOK

◯ ◯ ◯ ◯

5.	key

◯ ◯ ◯ ◯

6.	jeep

◯ ◯ ◯ ◯

Counts Syllables in Words

Objective:

Student counts the number of syllables (parts) in a given word.

Materials:

Mat, p. 107

Picture Cards, Set 1, p. 109

Picture Cards, Set 2, p. 111

Class Checklist, p. 113

Activity Sheet, p. 114

You may wish to use the Set 2 picture cards (moon, chair, flower, spider, kangaroo, elephant) for retesting purposes.

Model the Task

Place the mat on the table. Put the set 1 picture cards in numerical order and place them in a pile. Say:

> Today we are going to count word parts. Word parts are also called *syllables*. Let's begin.

Place the baby picture card on the table. Say:

> *Baby.* Listen for the word parts in *baby.*
> (ba)•(by)
> Two. There are two word parts in *baby.*

Place the picture of the baby in the number 2 row on the mat. Say:

> So I put the card in the number 2 row.

Student Task

> Now it's your turn.

Place the picture of the book on the table. Say:

> *Book.* How many word parts are in *book*?

Student responds. Say:

> Place the card on the mat next to the number.

Record the student's response on the class checklist. Place the pencil picture card on the table. Say:

> *Pencil.* How many word parts are in *pencil*?

Student responds. Say:

> Place the card on the mat next to the number.

Repeat the procedure and the script modeled above for each of the remaining picture cards. You may wish to use the Set 2 picture cards for retesting purposes.

Counts Syllables in Words

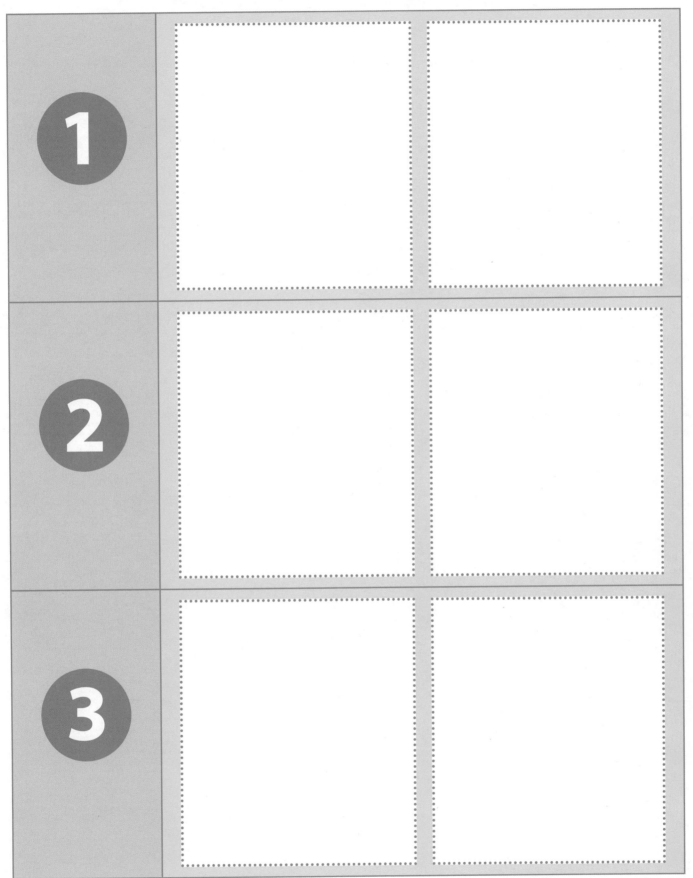

Counts Syllables in Words

1.

2.

3.

4.

5.

6.

Set 1
**Counts Syllables
in Words**
Phonemic Awareness

EMC 3337 • © Evan-Moor Corp.

Set 1
**Counts Syllables
in Words**
Phonemic Awareness

EMC 3337 • © Evan-Moor Corp.

Set 1
**Counts Syllables
in Words**
Phonemic Awareness

EMC 3337 • © Evan-Moor Corp.

Set 1
**Counts Syllables
in Words**
Phonemic Awareness

EMC 3337 • © Evan-Moor Corp.

Set 1
**Counts Syllables
in Words**
Phonemic Awareness

EMC 3337 • © Evan-Moor Corp.

Set 1
**Counts Syllables
in Words**
Phonemic Awareness

EMC 3337 • © Evan-Moor Corp.

Set 2
**Counts Syllables
in Words**
Phonemic Awareness

EMC 3337 • © Evan-Moor Corp.

Set 2
**Counts Syllables
in Words**
Phonemic Awareness

EMC 3337 • © Evan-Moor Corp.

Set 2
**Counts Syllables
in Words**
Phonemic Awareness

EMC 3337 • © Evan-Moor Corp.

Set 2
**Counts Syllables
in Words**
Phonemic Awareness

EMC 3337 • © Evan-Moor Corp.

Set 2
**Counts Syllables
in Words**
Phonemic Awareness

EMC 3337 • © Evan-Moor Corp.

Set 2
**Counts Syllables
in Words**
Phonemic Awareness

EMC 3337 • © Evan-Moor Corp.

Counts Syllables in Words

Class Checklist		Key: + correct response − incorrect response ● self-corrected					
Name	Date	book (1)	pencil (2)	pig (1)	butterfly (3)	telephone (3)	Notes

Name _____

Clap and Count

Name each picture. Clap the word parts.
Glue each picture under the number of claps you hear.

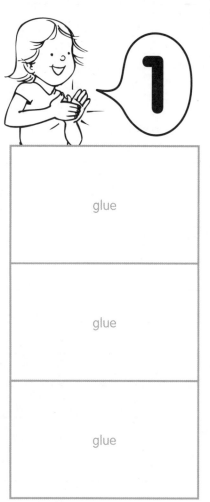

glue

glue

glue

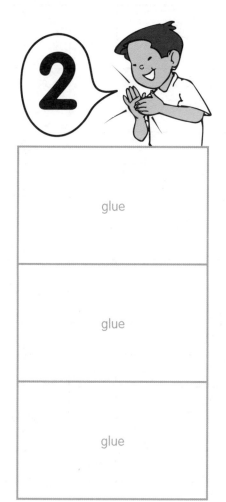

glue

glue

glue

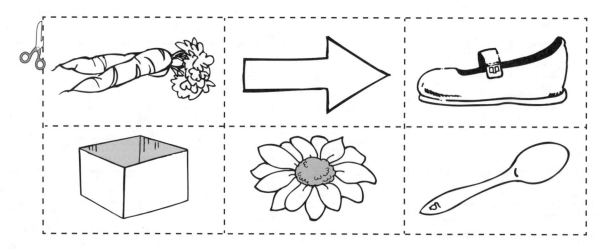

Quick Checks

Unit 3
Phonics and Word Recognition

Identifies Consonant Names and Sounds

Objective:
Student names each consonant and each consonant sound.

Materials:
Consonant Cards, pp. 119–123

Class Checklist, p. 125

Activity Sheet, p. 126

Student Task

Put the consonant cards in numerical order. Place card 1 on the table. Say:

> I will point to a letter on the card and you tell me what letter it is and what sound it makes. Let's begin.

Point to the letter *f*. Say:

> What letter is this?

Student responds. Say:

> What sound does it make?

Record any misidentified letter names or sounds on the class checklist. Point to the letter *l*. Say:

> What letter is this?

Student responds. Say:

> What sound does it make?

Point to the letter *m*. Say:

> What letter is this?

Student responds. Say:

> What sound does it make?

Remove card 1 and place card 2 on the table.

Repeat the procedure and the script modeled above for the remaining consonant cards.

Phonics and Word Recognition

3.

t

p

c

n

r

s

2.

f

l

m

1.

Identifies Consonant Names and Sounds

Phonics and Word Recognition

EMC 3337 • © Evan-Moor Corp.

Identifies Consonant Names and Sounds

Phonics and Word Recognition

EMC 3337 • © Evan-Moor Corp.

Identifies Consonant Names and Sounds

Phonics and Word Recognition

EMC 3337 • © Evan-Moor Corp.

6.

q

z

x

5.

w

b

y

4.

h

v

k

Identifies Consonant
Names and Sounds

Phonics and Word Recognition

EMC 3337 • © Evan-Moor Corp.

Identifies Consonant
Names and Sounds

Phonics and Word Recognition

EMC 3337 • © Evan-Moor Corp.

Identifies Consonant
Names and Sounds

Phonics and Word Recognition

EMC 3337 • © Evan-Moor Corp.

Phonics and Word Recognition

7.

d | j | g

**Identifies Consonant
Names and Sounds**

Phonics and Word Recognition

EMC 3337 • © Evan-Moor Corp.

Identifies Consonant Names and Sounds

Class Checklist		List any misidentified letter names. List any misidentified letter sounds.		
Name	Date	Letter Names	Letter Sounds	Notes

Name _____

Consonants

Point to each letter.
Name the letter. Then say the sound.

b   c   d   f   g

h   j   k   l   m

n   p   q   r   s

t   v   w   x   y

z

Hooray!

I know each letter name and sound!

Matches Short Vowel Sound to the Letter

Objective:
Student matches an orally stated short vowel sound to the correct letter.

Materials:
Vowel Cards, p. 129

Class Checklist, p. 131

Activity Sheet, p. 132

Setup:
Tape each vowel card to a craft stick.

Student Task

Place the vowel cards faceup on the table. Say:

> I will say a short vowel sound and you will choose the correct letter. Let's begin.
>
> Hold up the letter that says /a/ like in *cat*.

Student responds. Record the student's response on the class checklist. Say:

> Hold up the letter that says /e/ like in *bed*.

Student responds. Record the student's response. Say:

> Hold up the letter that says /i/ like in *pig*.

Student responds. Record the student's response. Say:

> Hold up the letter that says /o/ like in *box*.

Student responds. Record the student's response. Say:

> Hold up the letter that says /u/ like in *fun*.

Student responds. Record the student's response.

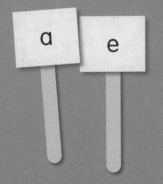

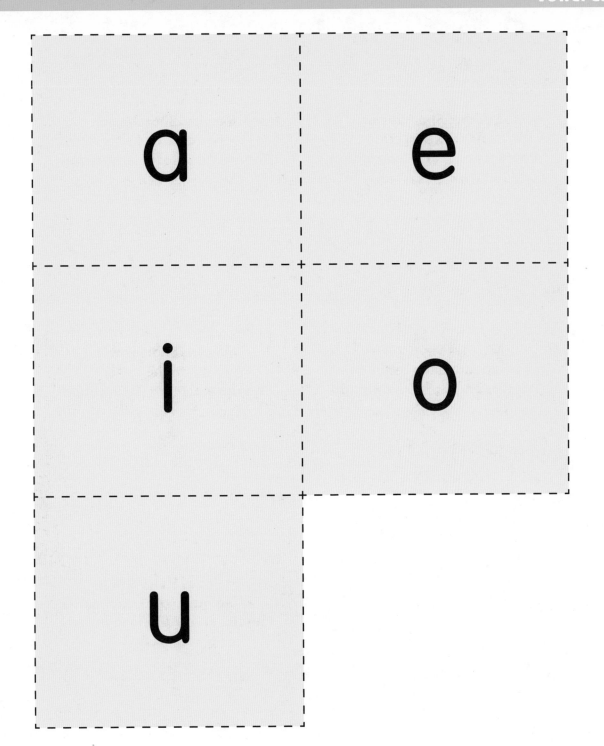

Phonics and Word Recognition
Matches Short Vowel Sound to the Letter **129**

**Matches Short Vowel
Sound to the Letter**
Phonics and Word Recognition

EMC 3337 • © Evan-Moor Corp.

**Matches Short Vowel
Sound to the Letter**
Phonics and Word Recognition

EMC 3337 • © Evan-Moor Corp.

**Matches Short Vowel
Sound to the Letter**
Phonics and Word Recognition

EMC 3337 • © Evan-Moor Corp.

**Matches Short Vowel
Sound to the Letter**
Phonics and Word Recognition

EMC 3337 • © Evan-Moor Corp.

**Matches Short Vowel
Sound to the Letter**
Phonics and Word Recognition

EMC 3337 • © Evan-Moor Corp.

Matches Short Vowel Sound to the Letter

Class Checklist	Key:	**+** correct response	**–** incorrect response	**●** self-corrected

Name	Date	ă	ĕ	ĭ	ŏ	ŭ	Notes

Name _____

Which Vowel?

Name each picture.
Circle the vowel sound you hear in the middle.

1. a i	2. e o	3. e i
4. o a	5. u o	6. e u
7. a i	8. o e	9. i u

Matches Beginning Sound to the Correct Letter

Quick
Checks

Materials:

Mat, p. 135

Picture Cards, p. 137

Letter Cards, p. 139

Class Checklist, p. 141

Activity Sheet, p. 142

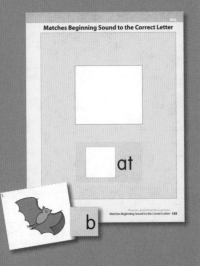

Student Task

Place the mat on the table. Hold the picture cards in numerical order. Lay the letter cards faceup on the table. Point to the mat as you talk about it. Say:

> Listen for the beginning sound in a word. Then choose a letter and place it on the mat. Let's begin.

Place the bat picture card on the mat. Say:

> *Bat.* Choose the letter that makes the beginning sound in *bat.*

Student responds. Record the student's response on the class checklist. Clear the mat and return the letter card to its group. Place the mat picture card on the mat. Say:

> *Mat.* Choose the letter that makes the beginning sound in *mat.*

Record the student's response on the class checklist. Clear the mat and return the letter card to its group. Place the cat picture card on the mat. Say:

> *Cat.* Choose the letter that makes the beginning sound in *cat.*

Record the student's response on the class checklist. Clear the mat and return the letter card to its group. Place the rat picture card on the mat. Say:

> *Rat.* Choose the letter that makes the beginning sound in *rat.*

Record the student's response on the class checklist. Clear the mat and return the letter card to its group. Place the hat picture card on the mat. Say:

> *Hat.* Choose the letter that makes the beginning sound in *hat.*

Record the student's response on the class checklist. Clear the mat and return the letter card to its group. Place the sat picture card on the mat. Say:

> *Sat.* Choose the letter that makes the beginning sound in *sat.*

Record the student's response on the class checklist.

Matches Beginning Sound to the Correct Letter

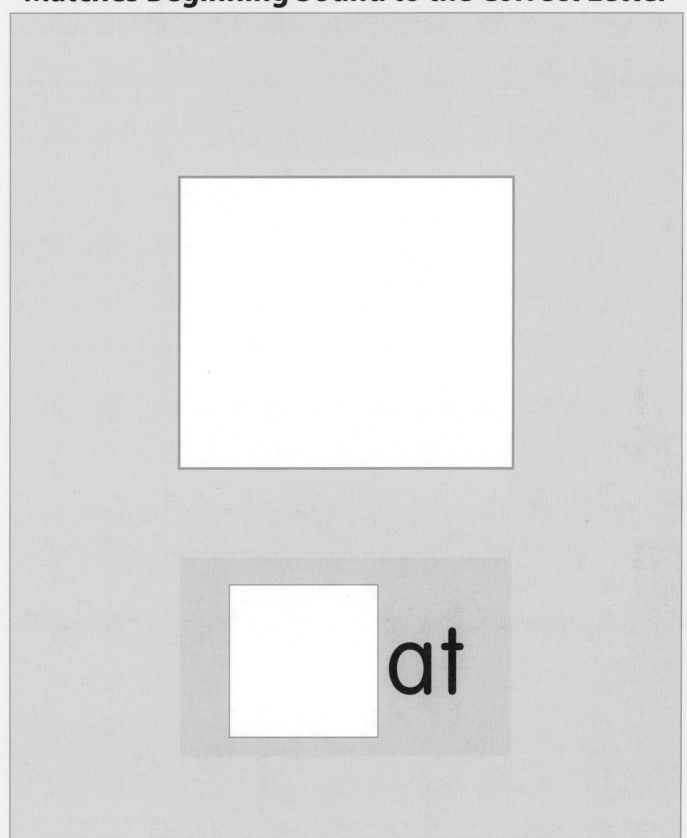

at

Matches Beginning Sound to the Correct Letter

EMC 3337 • © Evan-Moor Corp.

1.

2.

Welcome

3.

4.

5.

6.

Phonics and Word Recognition
Matches Beginning Sound to the Correct Letter **137**

mat

**Matches Beginning Sound
to the Correct Letter**
Phonics and Word Recognition

EMC 3337 • © Evan-Moor Corp.

bat

**Matches Beginning Sound
to the Correct Letter**
Phonics and Word Recognition

EMC 3337 • © Evan-Moor Corp.

rat

**Matches Beginning Sound
to the Correct Letter**
Phonics and Word Recognition

EMC 3337 • © Evan-Moor Corp.

cat

**Matches Beginning Sound
to the Correct Letter**
Phonics and Word Recognition

EMC 3337 • © Evan-Moor Corp.

sat

**Matches Beginning Sound
to the Correct Letter**
Phonics and Word Recognition

EMC 3337 • © Evan-Moor Corp.

hat

**Matches Beginning Sound
to the Correct Letter**
Phonics and Word Recognition

EMC 3337 • © Evan-Moor Corp.

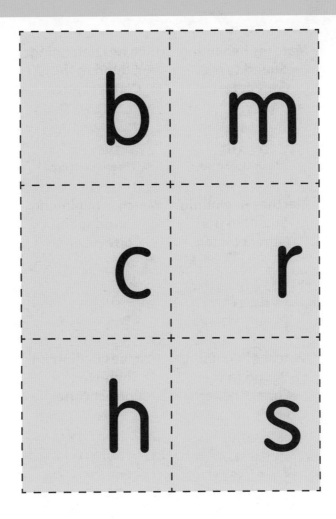

**Matches Beginning
Sound to the
Correct Letter**

Phonics and Word
Recognition

EMC 3337
© Evan-Moor Corp.

**Matches Beginning
Sound to the
Correct Letter**

Phonics and Word
Recognition

EMC 3337
© Evan-Moor Corp.

**Matches Beginning
Sound to the
Correct Letter**

Phonics and Word
Recognition

EMC 3337
© Evan-Moor Corp.

**Matches Beginning
Sound to the
Correct Letter**

Phonics and Word
Recognition

EMC 3337
© Evan-Moor Corp.

**Matches Beginning
Sound to the
Correct Letter**

Phonics and Word
Recognition

EMC 3337
© Evan-Moor Corp.

**Matches Beginning
Sound to the
Correct Letter**

Phonics and Word
Recognition

EMC 3337
© Evan-Moor Corp.

Matches Beginning Sound to the Correct Letter

Class Checklist		Key: + correct response — incorrect response • self-corrected						
Name	Date	Matches /b/ to b	Matches /m/ to m	Matches /c/ to c	Matches /r/ to r	Matches /h/ to h	Matches /s/ to s	Notes

Note: Student looks at each picture and writes the letter that represents the beginning sound.

Name _____

-at Words

Look at each picture.
Write the first letter of each **-at** word.

| b | m | c | s | r | h |

1.

_____at

2.

Welcome

_____at

3.

_____at

4.

_____at

5.

_____at

6.

_____at

Reads High-Frequency and CVC Words

Objective:
Student reads high-frequency and consonant-vowel-consonant words.

Materials:
Word Cards, pp. 145 and 147

Class Checklist, p. 149

Activity Sheet, p. 150

Student Task

Place the word cards in a pile on the table. Say:

> I am going to show you a word. Then you read the word to me. Let's begin.

Place the first word card on the table. Say:

> Read the word to me.

Student responds. If the student responds incorrectly or does not know the word, record the word on the class checklist.

Remove the word card and place it facedown. Draw another word card and place it in front of the student. Say:

> Read the word to me.

Student responds. Repeat the procedure and the script modeled above for the remaining word cards. Record any incorrect responses or words the student does not know.

EMC 3337 • Reading Assessment Tasks • © Evan-Moor Corp.

I	see	my
like	to	and
go	here	have
are	he	the
for	is	at

**Reads High-
Frequency and
CVC Words**

Phonics and Word Recognition

EMC 3337 • © Evan-Moor Corp.

**Reads High-
Frequency and
CVC Words**

Phonics and Word Recognition

EMC 3337 • © Evan-Moor Corp.

**Reads High-
Frequency and
CVC Words**

Phonics and Word Recognition

EMC 3337 • © Evan-Moor Corp.

**Reads High-
Frequency and
CVC Words**

Phonics and Word Recognition

EMC 3337 • © Evan-Moor Corp.

**Reads High-
Frequency and
CVC Words**

Phonics and Word Recognition

EMC 3337 • © Evan-Moor Corp.

**Reads High-
Frequency and
CVC Words**

Phonics and Word Recognition

EMC 3337 • © Evan-Moor Corp.

**Reads High-
Frequency and
CVC Words**

Phonics and Word Recognition

EMC 3337 • © Evan-Moor Corp.

**Reads High-
Frequency and
CVC Words**

Phonics and Word Recognition

EMC 3337 • © Evan-Moor Corp.

**Reads High-
Frequency and
CVC Words**

Phonics and Word Recognition

EMC 3337 • © Evan-Moor Corp.

**Reads High-
Frequency and
CVC Words**

Phonics and Word Recognition

EMC 3337 • © Evan-Moor Corp.

**Reads High-
Frequency and
CVC Words**

Phonics and Word Recognition

EMC 3337 • © Evan-Moor Corp.

**Reads High-
Frequency and
CVC Words**

Phonics and Word Recognition

EMC 3337 • © Evan-Moor Corp.

**Reads High-
Frequency and
CVC Words**

Phonics and Word Recognition

EMC 3337 • © Evan-Moor Corp.

**Reads High-
Frequency and
CVC Words**

Phonics and Word Recognition

EMC 3337 • © Evan-Moor Corp.

**Reads High-
Frequency and
CVC Words**

Phonics and Word Recognition

EMC 3337 • © Evan-Moor Corp.

cat	sit	mop
bed	tub	sun
fox	cab	leg
bug	fan	web
gas	van	mad

Reads High-
Frequency and
CVC Words

Phonics and Word Recognition

EMC 3337 • © Evan-Moor Corp.

Reads High-
Frequency and
CVC Words

Phonics and Word Recognition

EMC 3337 • © Evan-Moor Corp.

Reads High-
Frequency and
CVC Words

Phonics and Word Recognition

EMC 3337 • © Evan-Moor Corp.

Reads High-
Frequency and
CVC Words

Phonics and Word Recognition

EMC 3337 • © Evan-Moor Corp.

Reads High-
Frequency and
CVC Words

Phonics and Word Recognition

EMC 3337 • © Evan-Moor Corp.

Reads High-
Frequency and
CVC Words

Phonics and Word Recognition

EMC 3337 • © Evan-Moor Corp.

Reads High-
Frequency and
CVC Words

Phonics and Word Recognition

EMC 3337 • © Evan-Moor Corp.

Reads High-
Frequency and
CVC Words

Phonics and Word Recognition

EMC 3337 • © Evan-Moor Corp.

Reads High-
Frequency and
CVC Words

Phonics and Word Recognition

EMC 3337 • © Evan-Moor Corp.

Reads High-
Frequency and
CVC Words

Phonics and Word Recognition

EMC 3337 • © Evan-Moor Corp.

Reads High-
Frequency and
CVC Words

Phonics and Word Recognition

EMC 3337 • © Evan-Moor Corp.

Reads High-
Frequency and
CVC Words

Phonics and Word Recognition

EMC 3337 • © Evan-Moor Corp.

Reads High-
Frequency and
CVC Words

Phonics and Word Recognition

EMC 3337 • © Evan-Moor Corp.

Reads High-
Frequency and
CVC Words

Phonics and Word Recognition

EMC 3337 • © Evan-Moor Corp.

Reads High-
Frequency and
CVC Words

Phonics and Word Recognition

EMC 3337 • © Evan-Moor Corp.

Reads High-Frequency and CVC Words

Class Checklist			
Name	Date	Words the Student Cannot Read	Notes

Activity Sheet

Name _____

Words to Know

Practice reading these words.

I	see	my
like	to	and
go	here	have
are	he	cat
sit	bed	mop

Checks

Unit 4
Vocabulary & Concept Development

Understands Story Structure

Objective:

Student makes predictions about, answers questions about, and retells a story.

Materials:

Book: *Hide-and-Seek*, pp. 155–162

Class Checklist, p. 163

Activity Sheet, p. 164

Student Task

Say:

> I am going to read you a story, and then I will ask you some questions about it. Listen closely.

Read pages 1–5 of *Hide-and-Seek* to the student. Do not allow the student to view page 6. Say:

> Where do you think Sara is hiding?

Student responds. Say:

> Why do you think Sara is hiding there?

Student responds. Now read page 6 to the student. Then say:

> Tell me about the story. Where did we look for Sara first?

Student responds. Say:

> Were there any clues about where Sara was hiding?

Student responds. Say:

> Tell me what happened at the end of the story.

Student responds. Say:

> Now you hold the book and tell me the story.

Student turns to each page and uses his or her own words to retell the story. Once the student has finished, record the student's responses on the class checklist.

Hide-and-Seek

Vocabulary & Concept Development
Understands Story Structure **155**

My name is Sara.
I like to play hide-and-seek.
Close your eyes while I hide—don't peek!

1

Can you find me?
Look all around.
Look right and left, then up and down.

2

Am I in the kitchen, hiding by the sink?
Take a look. What do you think?

Am I in the living room, hiding near the chairs?
Or in the closet under the stairs?

4

Am I in the bathroom hiding in the tub—
where I scrub with a rub-a-dub-dub?
Look closely. What do you see?

5

Surprise!

You found me!

The End

Understands Story Structure

Class Checklist		Key: + correct response — incorrect response • self-corrected			
Name	Date	Makes Predictions	Answers Questions	Retells the Story	Notes

Name _____

What's Next?

Look at each picture. Draw what happens next in the story.

1.

2.

3.

4.

Sorts Items into Categories

Student Task

Place the mat on the table. Lay the picture cards faceup on the table. Say:

> Look at the mat. It has boxes for animals, boxes for toys, and boxes for people.

> Look at the picture cards and put each card where it belongs on the mat.

Student chooses a card and places it under a category on the mat. Student continues at his or her own pace until all the cards have been placed.

Use the mat with all the cards placed to accurately record the student's responses on the class checklist.

Objective:
Student sorts word cards into categories.

Materials:
Mat, p. 167
Picture Cards, p. 169
Class Checklist, p. 171
Activity Sheet, p. 172

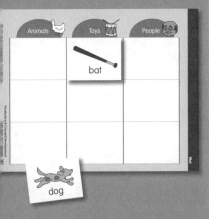

People

Toys

Animals

Vocabulary & Concept Development
Sorts Items into Categories 167

Sorts Items into Categories

Vocabulary & Concept Development

EMC 3337 • © Evan-Moor Corp.

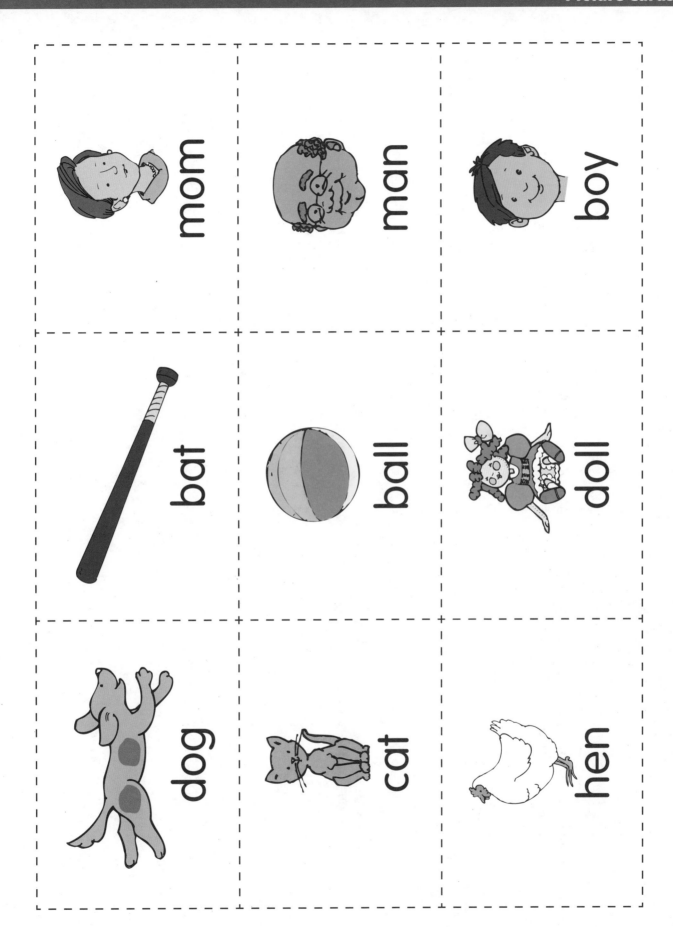

Sorts Items into Categories
Vocabulary & Concept Development

EMC 3337 • © Evan-Moor Corp.

Sorts Items into Categories
Vocabulary & Concept Development

EMC 3337 • © Evan-Moor Corp.

Sorts Items into Categories
Vocabulary & Concept Development

EMC 3337 • © Evan-Moor Corp.

Sorts Items into Categories
Vocabulary & Concept Development

EMC 3337 • © Evan-Moor Corp.

Sorts Items into Categories
Vocabulary & Concept Development

EMC 3337 • © Evan-Moor Corp.

Sorts Items into Categories
Vocabulary & Concept Development

EMC 3337 • © Evan-Moor Corp.

Sorts Items into Categories
Vocabulary & Concept Development

EMC 3337 • © Evan-Moor Corp.

Sorts Items into Categories
Vocabulary & Concept Development

EMC 3337 • © Evan-Moor Corp.

Sorts Items into Categories

Class Checklist	Key: + correct response			− incorrect response • self-corrected
Name	Date	Animals	Toys	People	Notes

Vocabulary & Concept Development

Note: Student categorizes words.

Name _____

Sort It

Cut. Sort. Glue.

Clothes	People	Animals
glue	glue	glue
glue	glue	glue